THE ROAD TO BECOMING A BETTER WIFE IN 21 DAYS

Dr. Shari Bowen

Copyright © 2026 Dr. Shari Bowen

All rights reserved.

No part of this publication may be reproduced, distributed, or transmitted in any form or by any means, including photocopying, recording, or other electronic or mechanical methods, without the prior written permission of the publisher, except in the case of brief quotations embodied in critical reviews and certain other non-commercial uses permitted by copyright law. For permission requests, email the publisher:

Attention: Permissions Coordinator

Welcome To The Storm Publishing!

info@w2tspublishing.org

Ordering Information:

Quantity sales. Special discounts are available on quantity purchases by corporations, associations, and others. For details, contact the publisher at the email address above.

Orders by U.S. trade bookstores and wholesalers.

Library of Congress Control Number: 2026928321

ISBN: 978-1-970822-03-8

Cover Design: Olaniyan Bukola

First Printed Edition: March 2026

Printed in the United States of America

Table of Contents

FOREWORD **4**
(By Apostle Randolph Bowen) 4

DAY 1 .... **6**
My Thinking, My Response 6

DAY 2 .... **14**
Activate Your Faith 14

DAY 3 .... **23**
Operate In Love 23

DAY 4 .... **28**
Operate In Humility (What About Me) 28

DAY 5 .... **33**
What Else Can I Do? (Bending Over Backwards) 33

DAY 6 .... **38**
A Life Of Prayer (Muscle We Don't Want To Atrophy) 38

DAY 7 .... **44**
Stand Still And Know (Let Patience Have Her Perfect Work) 44

DAY 8 .... **48**
Keep Focus On Jesus 48

DAY 9 .... **52**
The Package 52

DAY 10	**56**
Prefer The Other: Wife Posture	56
DAY 11	**59**
Talk About Him Good In The Streets: Bring Him Good Not Harm	59
DAY 12	**63**
Let Mercy Triumph Over Judgment (Pastor Ruth Jacob-Roberts)	63
DAY 13	**68**
Slow To Speak, Quick To Hear, Slow To Become Angry	68
DAY 14	**74**
Wise As Serpents, Harmless As Doves	74
DAY 15	**79**
Blessed Are The Meek	79
DAY 16	**82**
Gain The World Lose Your Soul? What's Really In Your Heart?	82
DAY 17	**86**
Purpose Driven—Use Zipporah: What's My Point?	86
DAY 18	**91**
Press To The Mark	91
DAY 19	**95**
Caught In Adultery	95
DAY 20	**101**

Believe God; Make A Room 101
DAY 21 .... **106**
To Moab We Go 106
About The Author **110**
Acknowledgements **113**
References **115**

FOREWORD
(By Apostle Randolph Bowen)

In my 10 years of pastoral education and seminary preparation, I have counseled many women concerning their roles as wives. I have found that many women (and men) bring a single-life mentality to a God-led and God-bred institution. Due to this institution being founded by God, the question of being a helpmeet is not up to humanity to answer. It is what God requires. God Himself started with, "Let us make man in our own image and likeness..." God prepared us, man and woman, for a union which must be realized through a disciple's life, or through a life dedicated to God.

From the standpoint of Ruth, we notice before she exhibited sacrificing her own reputation (her image, her character), she made herself of no reputation. She forfeited the idea that she was a beautiful woman who had it all together by gleaning in the field. What drove her there was the love and declaration that Naomi's God would be her God... so it is with marriage.

We must acknowledge God, decide to love, honor, cherish, and stand by one another in sickness and health, for better or for worse, till death do us part.

The art of marriage is in the choice. In this book, there is no magic pill. God is the foundation for marriage. The walls are built in humanity and the way we serve each other. Whatever material you use for the walls will determine the life of the structure, marriage in this case.

Remember, as you read this book, it is simply the thoughts of a woman who found out that after her choice to love this man for better or for worse, God's Word encouraged her to invest in a lifestyle of being a student and a disciple of Christ, so that her every action would be governed by God, not herself. I am truly blessed as an Apostle of the gospel that I found a woman who dedicated her life to God and made a choice to love (serve) me till death do us part.

DAY 1
My Thinking, My Response

Let us begin at the beginning. Before we can understand how to become better, we must first understand our original purpose. When God considered the creation of a being to address man's loneliness, His original design was to create a helper suitable for him (Genesis 2:18). This was not a secondary idea. It was intentional. In Genesis chapter two, verse twenty one, God caused man to fall into a deep sleep, stilling his conscious awareness. From man, He took a rib, a body part with regenerative capacity, and from it He formed woman. Adam then identified her nature and relationship to him, declaring, "This is now bone of my bones and flesh of my flesh" (Genesis 2:23).This statement defines purpose. It answers both the question of who she is and what she was created to be. After creating woman, God established the reason for her existence within the marital structure. In verse twenty four, God states, "Therefore a man leaves his father and mother and is united to his wife, and they become one flesh." This declaration clarifies function, order, and direction. The role is that of a suitable helper. The word suitable functions as the qualifier. It means right or appropriate for a specific person, purpose, or situation. It implies what is fitting, proper, and aligned with need. When God created woman for man, He did not create her lacking what the role required. She was formed with the necessary capacity, ability, and disposition appropriate to the level of performance demanded by helping. This was not incidental. It was built into her design.

What suitable is not: Suitable is not incompetent, inept, poor, unfit, unfitted, unqualified, improper, indecent, unbecoming, wrong.

Let us establish a foundation. There are several common thinking traps that many women I have spoken with over the years fall into when it comes to relationships. I have personally fallen into these same thinking traps as well. Before examining them individually, it is important to understand how thinking traps form. The human mind develops what are called schemas. These are mental frameworks that help us simplify and organize the vast amount of information we hold about people and situations, based on past experience (Robbins and Judge, 2019). Schemas serve a practical purpose. They help us predict outcomes and make decisions more efficiently, functioning as mental shortcuts that conserve cognitive effort.

Problems arise when these shortcuts take on a negative orientation. In the case of thinking traps, the schema becomes distorted. Rather than aiding clarity, it reinforces misinterpretation. Over time, this distortion becomes deeply ingrained. These patterns form through repeated exposure to certain experiences, how others behave toward us, and the situations we encounter. Once established, they influence perception automatically, often without conscious awareness.

What do we do with this information? Now that we understand God's original purpose in creating us, understand who and what He said we are, and recognize that our own thinking can produce an opposing narrative, we are left with several options. This is good news. The change required to begin the process of becoming a better wife starts with us. It does not begin externally. It begins internally. We are instructed to be transformed by the renewing of our minds. In Romans 12:2, when Paul tells us not to be conformed, he also instructs us to be transformed.

When this directive is given, there is no suggestion that someone else will complete this work on our behalf. The responsibility is personal. It is individual. And it is possible. We possess the capacity to change. At this first stage of becoming better, the most powerful tool identified at the starting point is knowledge. Knowing who we are. Knowing who we were created to be. And recognizing that if life and circumstance have shaped our thinking in ways that contradict that truth, we have the ability to correct it. With that understanding in place, we are ready to move forward.

How do I put this into action? What does this look like?

To step into my first new habit, I make up my mind to hold myself accountable for my thinking and my response. We are determined that faith is the prerequisite for success in any of the steps in this instructional guide to becoming better. Faith is in the power of God based on our belief in His Word. His Word says we have power to demolish arguments (cast down imaginations) and every pretension (high thought, opposing thought) that sets itself up against the knowledge of God, and we also have power to take every thought to make it obedient to Christ (2 Corinthians 10:5).

What this looks like in real life is this. When my husband shows love, or fails to show love in the way I expect, my initial response shifts. I now recognize the moment as an opportunity. I no longer default to my usual complaints or react by slamming or yanking objects in frustration. I take responsibility for my thinking and for my response. I interrupt the negative thinking trap of overgeneralization. I stop reacting with eye rolling, crying, or calling friends to describe him as heartless or inconsiderate. I stop posting on Facebook or sending public messages that signal his availability as a result of my dissatisfaction with his most recent action. I stop announcing to the world that he will never love me the way I believe I need to be loved.

I stop speaking in opposition to my faith, which teaches that love is patient and love is kind (1 Corinthians 13:4). Instead, I reverse my habitual thought patterns and respond differently. This is where I use the sound mind God has given me to examine the facts of what actually occurred. He woke up and reached for his phone, directing his attention to something other than me. He did not wake up, turn toward me, kiss my forehead, and tell me that he loved me. At this point, I am required to challenge the negative thoughts forming in my mind. My first responsibility is to address those thoughts before they escalate into an emotional state that leads to negative behavior. I pause. I think. I slow my response. I look for something positive in the situation. I thank God that we both woke up to see another day.

I thank God that he woke up at home, in good health, and unharmed. I praise God that he is here. Believe it or not, every husband does not come home every night. If this aligns with your situation, there is a process you can apply to regain control of your thoughts as well. In this space, my thinking and my response become more controlled, less emotional, and more aligned with who I am as a woman of God.

As I remain slow to speak and keep my mind focused on Him, remembering that He keeps me in perfect peace (Isaiah 26:3), improvement begins. I practice effective communication. I dismiss thoughts and behaviors that do not lead toward the promised life, or that take away from the abundant life Jesus died for me to have. I move into love. I become what I desire to receive. Some actions, and some desires of the heart, must be demonstrated before they can reasonably be expected.

Contrary to popular belief, desire alone is not enough. Our desires must be communicated. Often, expectations exist only in our own minds and are never expressed clearly. "I just want you to love me" is not clear communication. The way I want to receive love is not automatically understood. The calm. The peace. The unexpected response. These create the conditions for change. Now there is space to move forward. A new step can be taken to form a new habit, which leads to a new behavior. Now we can talk about faith.

Stay here as long as you need to. Get comfortable knowing who you are. Get confident in what God has spoken about you. If you don't know, find out. Read the Word. Link with a local, like-minded, God-fearing community. Get busy in gaining authority over your thinking. Get accountable in your response. You, woman of God, have the power and authority to direct your thinking, your response!

DAY 2
Activate Your Faith

Now faith comes by hearing, and hearing by the Word of God. But what is faith exactly, and how do I activate it? That is a fair question. The first step is understanding that faith has nothing to do with what we see. Difficulty understanding faith often begins with how we respond to sensation. Our perspective is shaped by how the mind interprets what we take in, sense, and perceive from the world around us. This raises an important tension. Where does faith fit? How do I unsee what I have already seen? How do I unhear something, or separate emotion and reaction from what I have already heard? The answer is not found in erasing experience. It begins with learning something new. Faith requires new input.

Creating a habit that activates faith starts with developing a habit that consistently brings the Word into my hearing. Today, tools make this easier than ever. Apps such as Bible Gateway allow Scripture to be read aloud while you drive to work, wash dishes, or sit quietly during the day. Read it. Listen to it. Have someone read it to you. The method matters less than the consistency.

The goal is to invest in hearing the Word. This is the foundation for faith to increase. Community also matters. Join a Bible study. Listen as the Word is explained and broken down for understanding. When Scripture is explained through the insight of a man or woman of God, it supports the ability to live by faith. Understanding creates alignment. I cannot act on what I do not understand, and I cannot live out what I do not know.

Along the way, I learned things about faith that I truly did not understand before. I once believed that as long as I asked the Lord for something, went to church when I was supposed to, listened to the preacher, prayed, and cried just enough, faith would automatically follow. Add loud prayers to the mix, and that was supposed to complete the formula. What I learned instead took me down a different path.

It led me to realize that I did not know God in the way I thought I did. One major piece was missing from my understanding. I had not fully accounted for the free will of others. Free will means people can choose. They can come and go. They can act as they please. Even when my intentions were sincere, and my expectations felt justified, free will still existed. I wanted to believe my formula would produce the outcome I desired, but it did not. What I came to understand is this. God is faithful to His Word. Even when people fail to honor their part of a covenant or uphold their side of a commitment, God does not stop being God.

At this point, I want us to pause and recognize something important. There are things we ask of God. I am not dismissing that. What I am explaining is how my understanding shifted when I began to see faith more clearly. When I speak about the free will of others, I am saying this. Operating in faith does not force God to answer my request by overriding someone else's ability to choose. Faith does not cancel the agency of others.

My understanding of faith was incomplete. God's faithfulness operates on a larger scale. Scripture tells us that all things work together for good for those who love God and are called according to His purpose (Romans 8:28). His faithfulness also assures us, "I will never leave you nor forsake you" (Deuteronomy 31:6).

The faithfulness of God assures us that there is nothing we can do to escape His presence. To overcome difficult times and operate in faith, I must gain wisdom. That requires learning and knowing the Word of God, because faith develops by hearing, and hearing the Word of God. This principle applies to all of us. To adopt the habit of operating in faith, investment is required. Faith grows through intentional practice and repeated exposure to truth.

It is helpful to break this down using a real example. I will use the topic of divorce. Since we are talking about becoming better wives, it makes sense to examine an outcome we do not desire and apply faith within it. In my first marriage, there was a day when my ex-husband came home and said that things were happening too fast and that he was leaving. It was Mother's Day. I want to pause here for clarity. Many of us place faith in the meaning of certain days, superstitions, or even perceived alignments. That is not faith. Faith is not rooted in symbols or timing. There is no connection to the Word of God in that way of thinking.

On this Mother's Day, after my ex-husband left, I entered a place of confusion, anger, sadness, and eventually blame toward God. I did not tell God that I was angry with Him. I did not tell Him that I believed this situation was His fault. Still, I went to God in prayer. I believed that if I prayed the right words, cried long enough, and added fasting, He would turn the situation around. This is where my misunderstanding of faith became clear. Before explaining what faith truly is, it helps to examine how I misunderstood it.

At the core, my heart was positioned in blame. I believed my situation was God's fault. Scripture tells us that the Lord requires us to come to Him with a broken spirit and a contrite heart (Psalms 51:17), and

He promises not to reject this posture. From the very beginning, however, I approached God believing He was responsible for my pain. There was another issue. I believed faith meant saying the right words. We live in a time where scriptures can be searched by topic and applied instantly. When this happened, that level of access was not available to me, but I did own a small book that listed scriptures for different life situations.

I began flipping through it. I took a notebook and wrote down every scripture connected to my heart's desire, asking and receiving, and anything else I believed God needed to be reminded of regarding my situation. To me, this was FAITH. I believed I was applying His Word correctly. I was convinced this approach would produce the outcome I wanted.

At the time, I believed the crying and fasting represented a broken spirit and a contrite heart. I was sincere. I begged and pleaded with God to change the heart and mind of my ex-husband, to make him return. What I was calling faith was actually an attempt to force someone else into my will. We can pause there for a moment. Often, we carry a packaged expectation of what we want the Lord to do for us. Rarely do we stop to consider whether our requests are aligned with the will of God. God's will has never been to force. Even in sending His only begotten Son, He allows us the choice to receive Him or reject Him.

What followed was difficult to accept. My ex-husband never came back. I left the covering of my local church and developed a deeply unhealthy attitude toward God and toward His people because my situation did not turn out the way I wanted. Have you ever been there? When disappointment sets in, we often redirect blame toward church people. In our minds, they are closer to God. If they are offering the prescribed solution, then it should work. When it does not, resentment grows. There was also truth I had to face about my fasting. It was not rooted in denying my flesh to pursue relationship with God. It was an attempt to pressure God into fixing my problem and bringing my ex-husband home by the end of the fast.

The faith I later learned to apply looked very different. Months before my ex-husband left, I heard a preacher, my own pastor at the time, say, "Some of your husbands are going to leave. Will God still be God?" That was a moment I should have paid attention to. Too often, when we hear the Word, we look around for who it applies to instead of receiving it personally. We search for someone else who fits the message, rather than hearing what is being said and applying it to our own lives.

Think about this for a moment. Have you ever sat in church, heard something powerful, and thought, "Someone else really needs to hear this?" What I should have heard and applied was this. The faithfulness of God means that no matter what situation we face, He remains sovereign. Hearing that truth without applying it kept me stuck. If I had applied it, it would have led me back to Romans 8:28, which says, "And we know that all things work together for good for those who love God, who are called according to His purpose." Over time, this became one of my favorite scriptures. Today, I hold God to that promise. As my perspective continues to change, I approach life with expectation rather than defeat.

To truly build a habit in this space, it requires us to apply God to every situation. Knowing and understanding His character helps us to apply His Word in correct context rather than applying one or two scriptures that match our own desired outcome. Faith throughout the situations we face means faith in the faithfulness of God. He is not a man that He should lie. So, if our outcome does not seem to be aligning with our prayers, we should consult a man or woman of God to ensure we have the correct understanding of the Word. Faith comes by hearing, and hearing by the Word of God... yet in all our getting (of the Wisdom of the Word), we must get an understanding.

DAY 3
Operate In Love

Love is patient. Love is kind. Love keeps no record of wrongs (1 Corinthians 13:4). What we know about love is limited. Often, we expect others to know more about us than we have invested in knowing ourselves. "I just want someone to love me the way I want to be loved" is a phrase I hear far too often. But what does that actually mean? Do you want flowers? Do you want quality time? Do you want words of affirmation or gifts? Some people say, "I just want to be together." Yet when you are together and the other person falls asleep, together alone proves to be insufficient. There is a method I learned recently. I call it the five whys. When I answer a question, I follow it with why at least five times. This process leads me past surface answers and down to the root. It requires honest introspection, and it ends with clarity. Let's walk through it so the process is clear.

First question: What do you want in a relationship? Answer: I want my husband to sit and listen to me when I talk, without interrupting.

First why. Because when I talk, it feels like he does not truly hear my side, and that makes me upset and withdrawn. Second why. I withdraw because I believe he is not listening anyway, and continuing feels pointless. Third why. I feel unheard often, and I avoid arguing because even during conflict, my perspective still seems invisible. Fourth why. I refuse to return to a place where I feel voiceless. When he cuts me off or does not listen, I react quickly, without concern for how harsh it may sound. Final why. As a child, I felt that my parents did not value or acknowledge the opinions of their children. Speaking up was not encouraged, so silence became my default.

These repeated questions led me to a fuller understanding of what it meant to be loved and, more specifically, to be heard. When we reach a deeper understanding of ourselves and the reasons behind our desires, it becomes easier to communicate those needs to others. We begin to understand the kind of love we are asking for because we are clearer about what we actually desire. I want to be valued. I want to be heard. This understanding connects to the scripture that instructs husbands to dwell with their wives according to knowledge (1 Peter 3:7). To obey that instruction and to walk in love in how we relate to one another, we must first have knowledge of ourselves. Who am I, and what do I truly desire?

This is only the first stage of forming a habit that operates in love. This smaller habit of self-examination builds personal understanding, which then helps others love us more effectively. It raises an important question about responsibility. What is my part? If I am patient with myself, it is only fair that I extend patience to others. Consider this: we have lived with ourselves our entire lives. If we do not fully understand ourselves, how can we fairly become angry with people who may not love us in the way we expect, when they have known us for only a portion of our lives? This is something worth reflecting on as we develop this new habit. What kind of patience am I willing to practice?

When we consider love, the key I have found is to measure it only by what the Bible says. Defining love in any other way usually prevents a single, agreed-upon, complete understanding. When we study 1 Corinthians 13, we become very familiar with what love is—and what love does. It is patient, kind, and keeps no record of wrongs. It does not dishonor, is not self-seeking, and is not easily angered. The critical point is action. Creating this habit of love requires tangible choices: the physical things I do, or the actions I intentionally choose not to take, because I decide to actively love instead.

The most challenging part I have noticed here is with keeping record of wrongs. It requires more than one of the new habits to step into a new space where active love is going to move forward in your role without counting the number of times your spouse does or does not do the thing you want. It is also important to note here that your active love is not dependent on your spouse's reciprocated or active love. In this process, it is most challenging when you expect to receive the same behavior back.

A perfect world says both individuals in marriage apply the self-help steps. Reality is it does not always work that way. The scripture tells us once we know to do good and do it not, it is a sin to us (James 4:17). In other words, I am accountable to the information once I am aware. If my spouse is not aware, is one of my acts of love to demonstrate it to them until they have a heart of mind to learn or try it for themselves?

DAY 4
Operate In Humility (What About Me)

Humility or submission used to feel like a dirty word. I did some reading and realized it is not as dirty as I once thought. It requires strength. It requires discipline. It requires understanding. Humility aligns with selflessness. Romans 12:3 speaks about not thinking of yourself more highly than you ought to. I have found this to be sound advice. This posture aligns with the character of Jesus Himself. Scripture instructs us to have the mind of Christ, and the passage continues by explaining that Christ had every right to be considered equal with God. Yet, because of His mission to die for us, even for those who may never accept Him, He did not take the credit He could have claimed.

Instead, He willingly set aside His status as part of the divine Trinity and came in human flesh. He became like you and me so that He could fully understand us and serve as our faithful and merciful high priest. That realization is striking. God's Son walked in flesh like mine so He could understand me and represent me. Yes, that is exactly what Scripture teaches. When we consider an act like this, an act of love, and then consider the role we take on as a wife, as one who is suitable and supportive, humility becomes unavoidable. It calls for honest self-examination. Do I love in the way I claim to love, or even believe I do? Am I willing to die to my own will for the sake of my spouse? As transformation takes place, operating in humility stands out as one of the most profound steps in the process.

Humility, by definition, does not mean thinking less of yourself. It means thinking of others more. That distinction matters. When we look at Jesus in the garden of Gethsemane, the weight of His mission is clear. It had become difficult, so difficult that He asked the Father to consider taking the cup, the mission, the assignment, away. Still, He reached the nevertheless, and that moment matters. In marriage, there are daily moments that make us want the Father to take the cup. In some marriages, this happens less often. In others, when it happens, it can take much longer to reach the nevertheless. This is where humility becomes practical rather than theoretical.

As we consider operating in humility, it helps to recognize how closely it connects with other steps. There is no way to operate in humility without first passing through love. There is also no way to operate in humility without faith, faith that God will supply all your needs according to His riches and glory.

This Scripture is often limited to provision such as food, money, or clothing, but it reaches further than that. God is also concerned with emotional needs. We see this in Luke 7, as Jesus entered the city of Nain. He encountered a woman He did not know, who was not asking Him for anything. She was a widow burying her son, and He perceived the cry of her heart. Compassion moved Him to act on her behalf. At this step, we must remove the question, what about me. Faith must operate at a level that trusts God to take care of me as I walk in obedience to this assigned role as a suitable helpmeet. Our suitability was spoken into being. It is our responsibility to walk into it.

I know the step of humility is difficult because our natural control + alt + delete is self-sustaining, self-protecting, and self-healing. Humility requires deeper selflessness. Humility and submission require me to act as Jesus did while completing His mission here on earth. Humility means that even when I want to argue my point because I believe I am right, I choose not to. You might ask, what if he is fussing at me, embarrassing me, or doing the same thing he always does again and again? Do I not get to retaliate? Humility means that even when I feel wronged, I do not have to seek revenge or try to balance the playing field. Can I speak truth to power? Absolutely. Even then, intent matters. Humility stands in direct opposition to pride.

Humility means I trust God with enough faith in His power that I am willing to lay down my own sword and stop operating in my personal protective strength. Humility is often mistaken for weakness. In reality, humility is a greater strength. It takes strength to recognize your own will, acknowledge the desire for it to prevail, and still choose to prefer another over yourself. That is strength.

DAY 5
What Else Can I Do? (Bending Over Backwards)

When we counsel married couples, a common theme emerges in conversation. Someone feels they are bending over backwards. They feel they have to do everything to maintain the house and care for the children. They wash clothes, manage laundry, and work tirelessly to keep the home running, yet feel unappreciated and unsupported by their husbands. Let me be clear. Bending over backwards is not natural. The position itself is abnormal. This step asks a question, but it truly requires a shift in perspective. Can I do my job? Can I do all the things I do, even without help? Is it possible?

Let us look at Mary and Martha. They were not husband and wife, but sisters. They shared a close relationship, yet their priorities differed at one specific moment. Mary sat at the feet of Jesus. Martha focused on cleaning and preparing the house for company. As we shift perspective, I want you to see Mary as your spouse sitting while you are bending over backwards. This requires a strong mental shift, but I trust you will stay with me.

Your Mary, or John, or Jim, or whatever your spouse's name may be, comes home from work to a home where you have been all day. You may have been home with children, alone, with a pet, or simply managing laundry and daily cleaning. Your spouse enters, possibly offers a light kiss, and instead of engaging in conversation or holding you for a few extra seconds, turns to a video game, changes your show, and shifts the atmosphere of the home.

Your attitude has been shaped by this game since the dating phase. It has always been your spouse's place of escape. At first, it did not seem like a serious issue. You assumed that once you were married, it would no longer matter. You see the twenty things you asked your spouse to do, which are still undone, as far more important than this game. From your perspective, the priority feels obvious. But I want you to step out of this imagined, yet very real, setup and consider what has been happening beneath the surface. This is something you have noticed for years. More importantly, this game functions as your spouse's route to calm. It is not random. It is not accidental. Shift with me for a moment. Mary sat at the feet of Jesus. By no means am I comparing a video game to the feet of Jesus. In her situation, she chose the thing that mattered most. Scripture makes this clear. For Martha, cleaning and being presentable held greater importance. If I know my spouse decompresses in a specific way, a different question comes into focus. What else can I do? Can I support the decompression? Can I become part of it?

Can we balance decompression by introducing a secondary method so that this one approach is not the only option? Variety and health work together. Often, we fight routines or norms we observe. The issue is not the game itself. The issue is the loss of attention directed toward us because of the game, or the friends, or whatever "feet" your spouse is sitting at while you are doing something else. In this scenario, your priority is not being questioned. What is being questioned is flexibility.

Can your approach be adjusted? Does cleaning always have to happen in one specific way? Can it move to certain days or times? Can it become a shared activity, maybe even paired with music? What else can we do? We often discover that we do not need to strain ourselves if we simply communicate and shift perspective. Shifting thinking is far easier than forcing effort in the wrong direction.

This step, as the first four, requires me as the wife to do something. You say, "I'm still bending even in following the step." If what I do is a chore, it will always seem as if I'm bending. If I am doing my reasonable service, the perspective will be different. One method I adopted in marriage goes back to Genesis 2 as God formed and presented Eve. She did not choose for herself which man to be with. Scripturally, we are reminded that the man who finds a wife finds a good thing and obtains favor from the Lord (scripture)... Even in that scripture, there is no action from the woman in the "obtaining phase." I, in turn, assume the position of suitable helpmeet as an assignment. I am on an assignment to help my spouse.

There are several things I must know in order to efficiently help. In addition, there are things that I will be required to do. If my attitude towards my husband shifts from serving or helping him to bending or accomplishing a task, I will not honestly be able to say that I am doing it all as unto the Lord. My perspective in helping demonstrates my heart posture.

If out of the abundance of the heart the mouth speaks, and my mouth consistently speaks to how much I am doing and bending, I need a one-on-one with the Lord to shift my heart posture. I often speak to ladies about the profoundness of being called and created as a helper suitable by God Himself. If we understand our being, our necessity, our roles... it would help us to operate in the role without being dismissive that an all-knowing God decided that we were required for His first creation, man, to be optimal. My bending has now shifted to an honorable and reasonable act of service.

DAY 6
A Life Of Prayer (Muscle We Don't Want To Atrophy)

I was introduced to a life of prayer not because I was a holy woman with a consistent relationship with the Lord. I was introduced to a life of prayer because every conversation with my husband felt difficult. There were important things I needed to say that were not being received. There were feelings I had about things he did that I could not share with anyone else.

I was carrying emotions I did not feel safe voicing. Frustration and difficulty, however, are never meant to tear down, paralyze, or stop the progress of a believer. Scripture reminds us to pray without ceasing (1 Thessalonians 5:16). I can pray. I can cry. I can do this throughout the day and still see no immediate results. A life of prayer is often adopted because someone has experienced the power of God through prayer and chooses to make it a lifestyle. Many people pray because they have been promised a reward, told something will change, or hope someone will be healed. Sometimes they pray simply to test it, because they are standing in a place of real difficulty.

This life of prayer in marriage is important to adopt as a habit because it supports every area of life. Prayer strengthens our relationship with the Lord. As with any relationship, the more I communicate, the more the relationship grows. One essential truth about prayer is that I must know what the Word says in order to pray effectively. Scripture tells us that we do not have because we do not ask, and that when we do ask, we sometimes ask incorrectly (James 4:3). If I do not know what God has already spoken, as written in the Bible, I cannot call it back to Him in prayer. When I pray, I am speaking with the Lord about what He has already said and applying it directly to my situation.

Contrary to popular belief, prayer is not always spoken. There are times when I pray in silence. There are times when prayer is simply thanksgiving, adoration, and exaltation. Reaching a place where, as a woman of God, I maintain an active prayer life means I am engaging with the Most High God daily. I am in conversation, a relevant conversation grounded in His Word, and there is nothing we cannot talk about.

Daniel's life illustrates this clearly. Throughout the book of Daniel, he demonstrates the ability to face any situation because of the relationship and lifestyle of prayer he had already established with the Lord. He did not begin praying in the lion's den. In Daniel 10, the angel explains that Daniel's fasting and prayer had already positioned his heart to understand, and the response came immediately.

Can you imagine experiencing good seasons and talking to God about them through thanksgiving? Can you imagine moments of frustration and bringing them to God, as Elijah did (1 Kings)? Can you imagine feeling weary and stepping away from the crowd to speak with the Father, as Jesus did in the synoptic gospels?

You see, a lifestyle of prayer is more dynamic than we often realize. It arms us with answers. It arms us with peace. Prayer arms us with patience. When my prayer life is intact, I am consistently engaging with the Word of God. In that place, I am equipped with a response for anything that comes against me. There was a time in my life when I asked the Lord to help me become the helpmeet He called me to be. I am still on that journey.

Through prayer, I discovered how much the Lord revealed to me about myself through His Word. Certain passages challenged me deeply, such as being quick to hear and not quick to reply. That was a recurring struggle within my marriage. So you see, a life of prayer equips us to course correct and to cover our spouse and children. This step matters greatly if we truly understand it.

Before I understood the power of prayer, my prayers sounded like this: "Lord, fix him." "Lord, help him stop treating me this way." But when this step is practiced correctly, something shifts. Your prayers stop focusing on changing the other person. Instead, they begin to include ways you can improve, because your goal becomes pleasing God. As the relationship deepens through consistent communication, you begin to recognize how much work remains in your own life. And trust me, when we start to improve, the relationship with our spouse improves as well. Our spouses notice the change. They notice the growth. Things begin to shift in our homes and in our lives. As we see in Daniel 10, from the moment we set our hearts to understand, He responds to our words. I dare you to try it.

The habit of prayer is our most powerful tool. Can you imagine owning a car, having the keys, yet not knowing how to drive? When we build the habit of prayer, we learn how to use the keys and maneuver the car. In my own life, I remember times when my prayers were toward the Lord as if He were a genie in a lamp. God desires a relationship with us, and our conversation through prayer is the direct line there.

The important factor is to learn what the Word of God says. God is faithful to His Word. When we learn His Word, our prayers are shaped using His own promises and principles. "It's me, oh Lord, standing in the need of prayer." I learn to honor God and prayer in the same manner Jesus taught the disciples in Matthew 6:9–14. After honoring God, praying His will, showing gratitude for what He has blessed us with, and asking forgiveness as we forgive others, we build the muscle of prayer and prevent attrition.

DAY 7
Stand Still And Know (Let Patience Have Her Perfect Work)

Standing still can be just as difficult as being quiet, especially before we understand why either matters. I continue to learn that our human, sporadic, natural response, what I refer to as control alt delete, is rooted in self-preservation. This means my instinctive response to offense, to events happening to me, whether good or bad, to pressure, and to difficulty is usually immediate. That reaction is rarely well considered.

It rarely reflects what scripture instructs me to do. So what is the significance of knowing that He is God? And why does patience matter so much? Let me share a moment with you. There was a time in my life when the Lord gave me advance awareness of something that was about to unfold. He told me He was placing me in harm's way, Afghanistan, in order to move me out of harm's way, a battle my husband would have had to face.

We were living in Germany during this time, and our marriage was about as rocky as an obstacle course in Colorado. When I look back on that season, I think about the many dynamics at play and how much confusion I would have added by forcing my presence. At a time when my husband was not clearly receiving from me, my loud voice would have been more disruptive than helpful. Many times, as women, we believe we have the right answer. We are confident in it, and we refuse to let the moment pass without making sure the room knows we know it.

Often, we are not wise in how we present our words. We do not always consider who the recipient is, how they process information, or the harm those words can cause if they do not land properly. I had to trust who my husband was in the hands of God. I also had to trust who God was, and still is, in my life. The Hebrew boys in Daniel 3 expressed it clearly: even if

He does not, He is still God. Our marriage faced struggles during that period that, under different circumstances, would have led us straight to divorce. But because of the foresight God gave me, despite the inconsistency, the fear, and the constant sense of life and death, I returned and spoke the same life over my husband that God had spoken to me.

I offered a gift of a glass plaque with Isaiah 11:2–5, reminding him of his own identity. During that phase of our marriage, I realized that while I had stood still long enough to know who God was, I was not fully certain of who my own husband was. Once I recognized that gap, I understood my role as a helpmeet more clearly. It did not take correction.

It only took a reminder for him to see and accept who he already was. Often, we become deeply focused on our relationship with God and forget to operate with the same awareness in our relationship with the human man in front of us. That man, in fact, needs to be reminded by his suitable helper that he is capable, that he can, that he does, and that he has access to anything he commits himself to believe.

The standing still is so real because in this step, you really feel your own hurt, your own pain, your own truth coming to life. It always will be a matter of choice. Do I focus on the real-life feelings and emotions before me, or do I focus on the truth of the matter which God has already spoken? Do I trust enough to stand still? Can I surrender my own will long enough for the things God has spoken to manifest? The truth is some days it works perfectly; some days it doesn't. Some situations, standing still and watching God is a piece of cake; other days, it brings about the true anger that sometimes wants to allow silence to impose. Who we are is not dictated by circumstances. Standing still proves our faith in our God! Give yourself grace. You can do this one.

DAY 8
Keep Focus On Jesus

He is the author and finisher of our faith (Hebrews 12:2). He keeps in perfect peace those whose eyes remain fixed on Him (Isaiah 26:3). It is fitting that this step follows standing still. In practice, the two often work together. Have you ever noticed someone standing still while staring into space? Standing still is ineffective if we lose focus on who Jesus is.

I often return to the example Jesus Himself gave as He stayed focused on His mission. In the book of John, Jesus is having a conversation with Peter. Let us place ourselves in that moment. Jesus, whom Peter had denied only chapters earlier, is walking with him and asking direct questions about love and commitment. Pause here and insert our own lives. When have we experienced an offense that no one addressed? When has something violated the rules of the home, yet no one raised the issue in order to keep the peace?

This is the space where Jesus and Peter were standing. Jesus did not revisit Peter's denial. He did not spend time rehearsing the failure, because that moment had already passed. Even more telling, Jesus had known it would happen and spoke of it before it ever did.

This is a serious point. There are moments in our relationships when we assume our spouse's behavior, and that assumption is not rooted in positive intent. Once a negative assumption forms, our behavior begins to align with it. That pattern is dangerous. Jesus spoke truth about Peter, but the difference between Jesus and us is this: Jesus did not mirror that truth with negative behavior. He did not treat Peter according to the failure He knew was coming. He spoke because it was true, not because He intended to react to it. Jesus understood Peter's character. In the Gospel of John, we see Jesus in a one on one conversation with Peter. We are still talking about marriage here. In addition to knowing Peter would deny Him, Jesus also knew the other prophecy: "Upon you, Peter, I will build my church" (Matthew 16:18).

This is the critical point. The denial did not cancel the future role. In our relationships, we often become so fixed on the offense that we cannot move past it into what lies ahead. In this conversation, Jesus asked Peter if he loved Him. Peter's emotions, much like ours, took offense at the question. Emotions are the fastest way for our focus to shift from Jesus to the situation. Jesus continued engaging Peter, and Peter responded by asking, "What about John?" This reveals another pressure point. Concern over what others will say or think often drives our reactions. It pulls our attention away from Jesus because waiting on Him feels too slow.

If, as a wife, I can keep my focus on the things of Christ, if I can prevent tone, body language, denial, or even betrayal, however it may be defined, from shifting that focus, I increase my ability to operate in the things of God. When my focus remains there, I am more likely to operate in forgiveness, because my attention is fixed on the ultimate forgiver.

Consider this example. On the cross, immediately after being spat on, mocked, and crowned with thorns, Jesus, fully focused on His mission, prayed, "Father, forgive them." Can you see yourself extending forgiveness immediately after being hurt?

The practicality of what Day 8 calls for will lead many to flip past this day and move on to something more realistic. The maturity Day 8 calls for will allow growth and development beyond your very own imagination. Many of us Christian folk say, "I'm going to pray about it and wait on God." Day 8 offers an action you and I can perform.

I focus on Jesus by focusing on His spoken Word, the examples of outcomes I already experienced, times when He already showed up (even when I was too immature to understand just how permanently He had my back), testimonies of others and my own, and mostly the faithfulness of our God! To focus on Jesus, I have to remember who and how I was and recognize the change happening in me because of Him. If He can do it for me... He can do it for anyone.

DAY 9
The Package

One of my greatest discoveries in this life was realizing that the package I expected was not the package I actually needed. When I understood that the package meeting my expectations might not contain what was required to care for me well, it was eye opening. I know that can sound unclear, so let me say it another way. My eyes can enjoy seeing tall, dark, and handsome. My hand can enjoy being held by a 6'2" individual with a slender build, wearing the scent of Cool Water. That may be the package I desire.

But I may not immediately recognize the package that holds the deeper contents. A heart that loves me fully. Patience for my proclivities. The intellect to carry a meaningful conversation. And a soul rooted in the love of the Father. That package may come in a 5'7" frame, with an island accent, and its own bumps and bruises. And that packaging may be exactly what fits me. Consider how many movies we have seen that present a list of what kind of spouse a woman should want. Consider the examples we grew up with, or the absence of examples that might have offered a reference point. The package is often shaped by society.

When I choose to be a woman of God, when I decide to be a godly wife, my focus shifts from optics to heart. The packaging is less important. That said, this does not mean disregarding presentation entirely. We must remain aware of how we present ourselves. Frankly, some people will not listen to or engage with someone who is not well presented. This is part of the same psychology that shapes our perception of the package we expect in a spouse. Scripture offers a clear illustration in 1 Samuel 16, when Samuel goes to anoint David.

Our natural response is drawn to the outer shell. Samuel focused on appearance, height, and other visible traits—the very traits that often cause us to overlook what truly matters beneath the surface. The exterior is easily seen, and because of that accessibility, we tend to invest effort into making it shine. I shared earlier that I am a veteran. Many years ago, our black boots were part of a nightly routine: we polished them until our reflection appeared on the leather. Shining boots did not require skill, but it demanded work, time, and patience.

There was a product called Leather Luster. Leather Luster took only a fraction of the time and left boots with a glossy finish that almost seemed too good to be true. Does this sound familiar? Young soldiers, single parents, or partying soldiers who spent their time elsewhere would grab Leather Luster for a quick once-over, readying their boots for work.

Soldiers who took pride in their uniform, however, would spend hours using elbow grease to shine their boots to perfection. The important point here is the outcome. Leather Luster's effect was short-lived compared to the lasting result of time, effort, and energy applied through natural strength. In marriage, what appears perfectly polished may still require the same natural strength, energy, and effort to endure.

Even after a few wears, Leather Luster would crack. The metaphor shifts us from the superficial premonition Samuel used to the deeper judgment of Jesus, who said He does not look at the outside but at the heart (1 Samuel 16:7). In marriage, our priority must not be merely observing the exterior and making decisions based on appearances. Instead, we must see, recognize what is truly present, and show gratitude for the package.

I am a strong believer that there is someone for everyone. It's interesting as a mother to look at the choices my children have made in relationships. When you consider your own personality, character, attitude, consider what package is necessary to have mercy, to show love, to extend grace.

This action will help with gratitude. When I can understand my spouse has qualities that would fuss with frustration rather than hit with malicious anger, my perspective changes, and I can show gratitude for my package. The package helps me look at myself, give close attention to what my response would be when dealing with myself... and this humbling moment produces gratitude for the package.

DAY 10
Prefer The Other: Wife Posture

Scripture tells us to love and prefer others above ourselves. Life and experience have taken me on a rollercoaster that has brought me to a place of selflessness. I continue to learn to prefer others—specifically my spouse—above myself. Philippians 2 instructs us to operate in humility, valuing others above ourselves. It is a true "aha" moment when the breakthrough from "what about me" finally occurs. Becoming a better wife based on biblical principles naturally leads to this humble, lowly place.

Where I often encounter resistance is when people focus on their own comfort. Remember, I was on this journey with the Lord, and my question to Him was, "How do I live out being a suitable helpmeet?" I was not asking how to get my husband to pay more attention to me, or to recognize my needs, nor was I asking how to be acknowledged after working hard. The position I brought to the Lord was one of self-responsibility and accountability.

Some readers, even at this point in the book, may feel they are doing most things right. Marriage is not about whether you are doing most things right. Nobody is really keeping score like that. The times we think we are right are based on our own perspective, which means our validity is limited by default. Wife posture means that under all circumstances, I will live up to who God created me to be: a helper, suitable for him (Gen 2:18).

When I get into a position to prefer the other, I cannot pull out a score sheet and recount the previous times I already preferred him. Furthermore, it is less about me. Humility is not thinking less of yourself. I can be humble while maintaining solid self-esteem. Humility is thinking of yourself less.

So, in situations where I could easily insert my feelings, emotions, or self-interest, I step back and consider my spouse. I prefer my spouse over myself. A tricky part of this step is that the first time it happens, it may go unseen. The second and third times may also go unnoticed. In reality, if the intent behind your action is to be seen, you are not truly operating in humility.

When we elevate ourselves to a place where our trust and hope are in God—to really be our Jehovah Jireh, our provider, Way Maker, Care Giver, and Protector—it means I will not stop preferring my spouse even to take care of myself. If I stop operating godly to take care of myself, I have acted faithlessly. Faith says, "I believe God will do it." Faithless means, "God hasn't shown up yet, so I will handle it myself."

Day 10 is practical, and though it sounds simplistic, it requires full awareness. Can I operate with self-awareness, truly experience a feeling, and thank God for the feeling while looking beyond the personability of the feeling and prefer my spouse above myself? Can I take into consideration that it will not be about me? Will my "self" intrude during this process to remind me of all the things someone should be doing for me? Have I had a conversation? Can I live past not receiving yet?

DAY 11
Talk About Him Good In The Streets: Bring Him Good Not Harm

How hard is it to say something good about anyone when you are upset with them? Stop for a second and think about that question. Yes, church folks. Religious folks. Do we not get upset? At times I get MAD!! This chapter is absolutely transformative if you can grasp it. How do we do this? How do we talk about someone god when they have just made us feel bad—without being fake? There is a key to this formula... SITUATION-SELF=GOOD IN THE STREETS (S-S=G)!

Whenever you face a situation, no matter how bad, if you remove the personal element, it becomes easier to speak well of the person publicly. If I can reach a place where I do not take offense personally, I can operate here. The gold is seen when Jesus speaks to a thief hanging on the cross. Or the woman caught in adultery. Or the woman at the well. Do you get the point? Everyone was flawed, sinful, or marginalized, yet the Sovereign Savior still found a way to communicate their worth. Proverbs 31 describes a virtuous woman who is a rare find.

Emotions often stand between us and understanding. Here we are again discussing emotions—they are a true dictator of our actions. This virtuous woman is able to bring her husband good and not harm. She can be trusted, and she enriches her husband's life. Do not assume this means the marriage is perfect. Consider all the work she is doing as described in scripture. In today's terms, this woman might be compared to one who "bends over backwards," but bending over backwards is abnormal. She is simply performing her reasonable service to be suitable. Powerfully and significantly, this woman does not even have a name.

This woman is you. This woman is me. When I think of conversations with women who feel used, overwhelmed, or unappreciated, I see a zeal similar to that of the virtuous woman in Proverbs 31—grit, hard work, determination, careful planning, consideration for her family, her resources, and those who depend on her.

Are we virtuous? Can we be? It begs the question: What am I here for in this marriage? Am I seeking recognition or reward? Am I striving to be a wife who pleases God? Am I carrying the name my husband entrusted to me, the legacy and honor of a bloodline I was invited to join? How am I doing that? Can I address my feelings without belittling my spouse? Can I offer my spouse good even when I don't feel good? Can my response to pain be love? Can I give the very thing I need, in addition to everything else I am already doing as a wife?

Day 11 asks some difficult questions. As this is lived, it can sometimes feel deceptive. The truth is that if we are operating in faith, we operate from a place where we speak those things that are not as though they are. We are fully expressive in terms of our feelings and needs. We are patient in affliction. We are diligent in our homes. Our children are not suffering because we are so sad in our demeanor that they perceive our sadness and behave reflective of that discomfort.

This is not asking us to be fake or inauthentic nor untruthful. This is provoking a next-level faith that can speak, and stand, and work, and wait on the mighty hand of God! I have lived the moments where I wanted to tell my leader how bad I was feeling. I remember in that moment I slowed my words and even shared with my leader, "Sir, I want to complain, but I am reminded that I asked God how to be a better helpmeet, and He reminded me... this is your chance." The message was to take the opportunities of pain, weakness, and discomfort and apply faith through the Word!

DAY 12
Let Mercy Triumph Over Judgment (Pastor Ruth Jacob-Roberts)

Marriage is a sacred covenant between two imperfect people, and mistakes and misunderstandings are inevitable. The biblical principle in James 2:13—"Mercy triumphs over judgment"—offers profound wisdom for navigating these imperfections. In a world that often encourages judgment and retribution, this truth reminds couples to embrace mercy as a guiding force in their relationship.

Mercy begins with understanding. Every spouse brings unique experiences, strengths, and weaknesses into a marriage. Instead of magnifying flaws or dwelling on shortcomings, mercy invites us to approach one another with compassion and grace. This mindset creates a safe space for vulnerability, allowing both partners to admit failures without fear of condemnation. As Ephesians 4:32 reminds us, "Be kind to one another, tenderhearted, forgiving one another, as God in Christ forgave you." Forgiveness is not merely a reaction—it is a lifestyle that sustains intimacy and trust.

To truly grasp mercy, we must understand its biblical depth. In the original Greek, the word for mercy is eleos, which means kindness or goodwill toward the miserable and afflicted, joined with a desire to relieve them. Mercy is not passive; it is active compassion that moves us to forgive and restore. It reflects God's heart toward humanity—favor we did not earn and blessings we do not deserve. This is grace in action.

The Old Testament gives a powerful image of mercy through the mercy seat, located atop the Ark of the Covenant in the Holy of Holies (Exodus 25:17-22). It was the place where God's presence dwelled and where atonement was made for sin. In marriage, the mercy seat symbolizes a sacred space where forgiveness and grace cover judgment. Just as God meets us at the mercy seat, couples must create a "mercy seat" in their relationship—a space where love and grace triumph over criticism and condemnation.

Mercy in marriage means choosing love when judgment feels easier. It means saying, "I will not treat you like something worthless because of your mistake." Instead, you extend favor your spouse did not earn and did not deserve—just as Christ does for us. This is the essence of grace: unearned, undeserved, yet freely given. Human love alone is limited.

We cannot truly love others as God calls us to without His love flowing through us. Romans 5:5 reminds us that "God's love has been poured into our hearts through the Holy Spirit." When mercy triumphs over judgment in marriage, it is because Christ's love empowers us to forgive, to show grace, and to choose restoration over retaliation.

Mercy also shapes the culture of marriage. Couples who prioritize grace over criticism create an environment where joy and harmony flourish. They celebrate each other's successes, express gratitude, and speak words of encouragement. Communication becomes gentler and more constructive, even during disagreements. Instead of harsh accusations, spouses learn to express feelings with empathy and seek understanding rather than victory.

Finally, mercy triumphs over judgment when couples let go of past grievances. Holding on to old wounds can poison a marriage, but mercy liberates both partners from resentment. Letting go does not mean ignoring pain; it means refusing to let past hurts dictate present interactions. By moving forward with intentionality, couples build a future rooted in grace and mutual respect.

Mercy transforms marriage into a sanctuary of love and support. It reflects the heart of God and enables couples to grow together in intimacy and trust. When mercy triumphs over judgment, the power of love flourishes.

Prayer for Couples

Lord, thank You for showing us mercy when we deserved judgment. Help us to reflect Your heart in our marriage. Teach us to forgive quickly, love deeply, and create a culture of grace in our home. May Your mercy triumph over judgment in every area of our relationship. In Jesus' name, Amen.

DAY 13
Slow To Speak, Quick To Hear, Slow To Become Angry

Today's step, like many others, is not a one-time or one-day activity. The title alludes to a lifestyle. It alludes to consistent, ongoing behaviors. Prayer is communication with God. It is speaking and listening. It is waiting. It is quiet, it is loud, it is constant. I once had an injury that required surgery. As I recovered, there were things I could no longer do the way I once did them. I could not run the same, nor could I work out the same. Some of my muscles experienced atrophy—a breakdown in strength due to lack of use.

Let's transition from exercise to communication. Have you ever felt that you and your spouse were not on the same page? Have you ever experienced conversations that were short, lacked detail, and felt so challenging that you stopped talking altogether?

Communication can behave like a muscle. There are times in marriage when we avoid certain subjects—topics that make us uneasy, or whose outcomes we assume in advance. When we do, we allow the "muscle" of communication to atrophy. I discourage this behavior.

I am not recommending something that comes easily for me. I am the first to raise my hand and say, "I don't like contention." That statement is a copout. The reality is that anytime two individuals interact, there is an opportunity for conflict. People are different. Marriage is supposed to be a safe place. We, the two of us in the marriage, can make it anything else. We decide how to talk, what to say, what words to use, what words to omit—the sharpness, the depth, the pain. When scripture instructs us to be slow to speak, it is teaching an art we must learn. Slow is not simply a measure of speed. Slow entails consideration, even compassion. Slow requires the humility we discussed earlier. Slow involves thought. Being slow to speak means my words will not be rash or harsh. The speed itself is not the point; it is the deliberate pause that allows me to act with responsibility. The art requires a dose of emotional intelligence.

This means I recognize my emotions, and from a place of self-awareness, I operate with responsibility and discipline. In keeping with emotional intelligence, I also pay attention to my spouse. I take time to understand body language. What tones am I hearing? Is there frustration? Where is it coming from? The art of slowness is understanding the situation fully. In the Bible, there is a story where Jesus walked into a town called Nain. He saw a woman and assessed the situation. He quickly moved from observation to compassion.

Slowness in speaking was preceded by consideration and care. Where is our heart in our marriage? Once I learn the art of being slow to speak, I can simultaneously develop swiftness in hearing. This may seem contradictory. My eyes see, I sense, I perceive, and then I speak. This instruction slows the normal patterns my brain has created for responding. I shift the quick response from speaking to listening.

The key is that as I hear and perceive in this manner, the vibrations are converted into signals my brain can interpret. As I recognize what I hear, I also recognize the origin. In marriage, it is crucial to understand my spouse to the level that reveals whether words are spoken with intent to hurt, to love, to care, out of confusion, in retaliation, or for another reason.

If I do not understand the intent, it is up to me to ask questions. If I do not make an effort to master not only my words, my lexicon, and my emotions—but also the emotions of my spouse, even during moments of discomfort in difficult conversations—the recommendation and habit suggested for Day 13 will be void. Being slow to anger is directly linked to how well I master being slow to speak and quick to hear. Slow to anger is the consequential behavior associated with how quickly I can replace judgment with compassion.

Think about this: when Eve faced punishment in Genesis 3 for eating the fruit, Adam initially cast blame. Yet when they were banished, they left together. They procreated after. In other words, even though his immediate response was blame, we do not see Eve fight back. The bottom line is that there is a time and place for every conversation and every response. The wisdom of being a godly wife, a better wife, is exploring this landscape and gaining understanding. Attaining and maintaining self-control leads to success.

My first attempt at consciously trying this step had me more upset than when I began. I suppressed instead of rationalized. I did not make sense or give value to what I was feeling. I thought if I held my tongue, that was enough. I thought if I kept my opinion to myself, that was being slow to speak. On the contrary. Like many of the recommendations, the answer is not suppression or dismissal of true feelings and emotions. Suppression led to an explosion.

Everything stayed covered up or hidden, until the tipping point was reached. The answer is in discipline to recognize and share those feelings at an appropriate time where they will be received, or listened to, and to be prepared for them to even be rejected. A huge part of learning one another in marriage is awareness of and respect for the level of growth or lack thereof your spouse is experiencing. Another golden nugget is that we are not always at the same place in development at the same time. Age does not equal maturity. Effective communication is the gateway.

DAY 14
Wise As Serpents, Harmless As Doves

Assessment is due diligence in marriage. Day 14 suggests that we are to be wise as serpents. In Genesis, the serpent is described as more cunning or crafty than any other animal God made. Both words imply the ability to use deceit for selfish ambition. By contrast, consider the dove. Some of its characteristics include speed, precision, strong navigation, loyalty to its mate, and—most importantly—adaptability, which allows it to thrive in diverse environments.

In Matthew 10, Jesus gave this instruction to the disciples, teaching them how to behave as they spread the gospel. The assignment in marriage is similar: a soul is at stake daily—two souls. I learned from my father that the person who can hurt you most is the person you love. Each individual carries expectations of what love is and of how someone who loves should act.

Being wise as a serpent builds on the understanding discussed in Day 13. That understanding must precede the act of discerning how to operate effectively with your spouse. Wisdom in relationships requires attention to everything we learn about one another. We come to know each other's deepest hurts, and some of us are fortunate enough to hear about one another's darkest fears.

We hear stories that draw us closer in our role of protecting and providing safety for each other. Yet there comes a time when our sense of self feels threatened, and in an effort to protect ourselves, we may use information that once invited love and grace to defend against one another. This action is hurtful, dangerous, and often difficult to recover from due to the betrayal it carries.

The dove—the adaptable, harmless dove—is the model we are encouraged to embody. Though we may have information that could be used to harm—and some of us have used it in the past—that information must be kept close and well-guarded. It is meant to teach us how to love and pray for one another, not to weaponize in defense. In relationships, we often try to make sense of one another's behavior, especially when it causes pain. I have heard phrases like, "That's why your ex-husband left you," or "No wonder no one will marry you." Consider how much time it takes to rebuild trust when words tied to past trauma are used to highlight imperfection. It is therefore essential that the wisdom gained from being slow to speak, quick to hear, and slow to anger is expressed through harmlessness. The knowledge we acquire should allow us to act with love and resilience.

Understanding my spouse's experiences with bullying, for example, helps me recognize the origin of certain words in pressure-filled situations. Harmlessness, applied alongside wisdom, allows us to discern when words are misplaced and not intended as attacks. Adaptability—the dove's characteristic—helps us maintain perspective, and wisdom guides our communication, fostering peace within our home.

I remember this played out as an irate husband yelled publicly about a very unimportant factor. If I remember correctly, it was a glass of water, bottle versus a cup at a restaurant. The furiousness in the tone and the frustration in the speech warranted retaliation. Think of all the dynamics at play. We are in public. People are hearing this and they are starting to stare. I could err on the side of embarrassment. When exercising slow to speak, I take in what's happening. I evaluate my emotional state, my level of consciousness and awareness. I start to consider what happened to create this environment.

I make eye contact and try to evaluate body language. I recognized a phone call just ended. The person with me comments on the aggression. In real time, this exercise did not feel great. I was quickly able to use wisdom to understand the frustration was from something else, so though the conversation seemed to be directed at me, it was displaced.

When we are on assignment in our marriages, it is important not to allow the opinion of the masses to infiltrate decision making. I quickly and quietly commented, "oh that's not for me..." and continued to ask how I may be of service. It's so necessary to remember *the baseline. Who am I dealing with and what are the triggers for this person. Am I aware of what causes or adds to frustration? What do I do with that information?*

DAY 15
Blessed Are The Meek

The word meek... I know we continue to revisit words such as humility, lowliness, and meekness. Day 15 continues to echo this posture. Meekness is central to the success of a better wife. In reality, the character of a godly wife—a helper suitable—is defined by her ability to respect and honor her husband. The meek shall inherit the earth. But what exactly is "the earth," and what does it have to do with marriage? The answer lies in the attributes of meekness: self-restraint. The strength required to exercise restraint is both powerful and gracious.

The restraint we exhibit as meek women reflects our trust in God's authority, His roles, and His promises. God's will and our ability to meet the needs of others come alive when a godly wife demonstrates meekness. The opposite of meekness is pride or arrogance. Pride says, "Because I can hurt you, I will."

Pride says, "I will make you feel the way you make me feel." The inheritance of the meek is the earth. How full is that promise? Psalm 24 reminds us that the earth belongs to the Lord and all that is in it.

Matthew 5 tells us the meek shall inherit the earth. When we understand that meekness involves controlling our own will, and we see the promise attached to it, the principle becomes clear: by exercising the same humility and self-restraint Jesus exhibited—taking on the form of a servant and making himself of no reputation (Philippians 2:6)—we inherit access to all that our Father owns. Jesus himself inherited the name above every name (Philippians 2:9). A little self-control goes a long way. Self-control may sound simple, but in practice, remaining in control is often far more difficult than acting out of control. And yet, it is a choice.

The question is, "Do I want the inheritance?" Is it worth it for me to maintain control of myself despite what I face or perceive in others for the sake of the inheritance?

The truth of the matter is that in the heat of the

situation I am not counting the cost of the inheritance. Honestly I bank on God's mercy and his grace! We must be transformed by renewing our minds to build a new reaction code. To decode and recode our mental path in a way that exercises meekness as a normal response is the key to success on Day 15. Practice it.

You will have ample opportunity to practice this because your spouse will engage in a conversation or an interaction with you and the first words that come to mind will not be meek. Those words will not be kind or thoughtful. What are you going to do? Can you operate in respect and honor without meekness?

//DR. SHARI BOWEN

DAY 16
Gain The World Lose Your Soul? What's Really In Your Heart?

Most of us like to think we are good Christians. Most of us believe we are typically good people. We do right by most, and we are kindhearted. We give to the poor by donating clothes, and we even put offerings in the collection basket when it circulates. Those are commendable actions. As a matter of fact, there was a young man in the Bible named Cornelius who operated in the same way, and he was considered devout. His giving reached God's attention so much that God sent a vision to Peter, preparing him to go to Cornelius' house and save his family and friends (Acts 10).

So what does this mean for marriage? I might think I have done most things correctly, with decent intentions. The truth is, there are times I have acted out of my own desire to say no. Sometimes I do things because I always do them, and this time I don't want to. Sometimes I act because I am a wife, not because I am serving with joy and gratitude. Here's a perspective to consider. The Bible says, "The man who finds a wife finds a good thing and obtains favor from the Lord." Imagine if we—the good thing—became so difficult that our husbands lose out on favor from God.

Imagine doing all the giving, serving the community, the children, the auxiliaries correctly—but in our closest relationships, our hearts are not grateful. Our intentions are full of malice, selfishness, and vanity. We become the center of attention. Cleaning is done with the expectation of thanks. A good meal is not prepared unless someone helps with the dishes afterwards. Every action is performed with an expectation of a reaction that validates us or makes us feel appreciated. At this point, we must ask ourselves: am I more concerned with the approval of people? Am I more satisfied with human gratitude than with the approval I could receive from above—by being a virtuous woman whose value is far above rubies?

I hear the Bible refer to people who do things to be seen as hypocrites (Matthew 6). The cheerful giver mentioned in 2 Corinthians 9 refers not only to the giving of money, but also to the giving of oneself, one's gifts, and one's love. When Scripture says we are known as God's representatives, His disciples, by the love we show one another, and yet within the four walls of my own home I struggle to show love, I am not in a good position. A grudge is what leads to the loss of my soul. When, as a wife, my actions are done grudgingly or out of compulsion, I understand that the same principle applies. Give grudgingly, reap grudgingly.

It is easy to place blame when looking outward. The choices we make often create a dwelling place for blame within. I found clarity in Romans 12:3b, which tells us not to think more highly of ourselves than we ought to. That verse settled deeply in me because the moment I realized my actions were not genuine or rooted in love, I had to confront the truth. I thought I was better.

I thought I deserved more. I had to consider the King, our Lord and Savior, who humbled Himself by clothing Himself in human flesh. Deity walking among us. I realized quickly that I had never done that. If asked to die for someone, except perhaps my children, I would stop short at, "Father, let this cup pass from me." I do not believe I would mature into the posture required to give my life and take on the weight of humanity's stain.

I remember being mad at my husband to the point where I did not want to look at him. I was disgusted and disappointed with his choices and disregard for my feelings. The truth of me feeling this way impacted every behavior directed to my husband. Every dish had extra slam. I would cook it, but it would lack a little salt. I would go pick up the laundry and fold the clothes, but it was with no intentionality.

Everything I did reflected nonchalant attitude and disregard for the man whom God said I would have respect for.

DAY 17
Purpose Driven—Use
Zipporah: What's My Point?

The purpose—the point—though it sits at the end, is important to know up front. What is the point? Why are you married? What is the goal? These are real questions when you consider what you are signing up for and count the cost. Are things always going to be this way? Is this way good enough? Do I believe change is possible? Are either of us willing to work for change? Do I wait for my spouse to change, or do I put forth effort first?

What is happening before my eyes? Am I enduring treatment until death? Am I willing to invest in this marriage to experience the abundant life Jesus came and died for me to have? What is my point? When I studied and read to prepare this chapter, I looked at the life of Zipporah in Exodus 4. The questions about the end should be our starting point. Consider many relationships we see: people still upset over actions from years ago. Couples we counsel sometimes lack genuine care for each other, but the financial convenience of marriage keeps them together. The individuals are unhappy, uncaring, and unconcerned about each other's future.

Put yourself in Zipporah's shoes. One day you go about your routine—getting water, buying groceries, managing your household—when a helpful man appears. He does things you have never experienced before. Kickstand moment here: we often get excited about something new, or something we never had, and call it love. We attribute the novelty of someone's actions to love. The danger is that we do not take time to understand the character of the person. Before we have a chance to gain our bearings, we can fall head over heels. The lesson: a new thing, a new way, does not equal love. Zipporah went home and told her father about the encounter, and shortly after, she married this man and began life with him. As you follow her story in your spiritual imagination, note that she referred to him as an Egyptian.

This is important, firstly, because Moses grew up in the house of an Egyptian, but that was not his heritage. Zipporah experienced something new and assumed his origin. This is critical because, in our marriages, many of us make assumptions about our spouses' backgrounds. Asking questions and understanding who we are dealing with—who their family is, what their heritage or family line believes, and what they stand for—are all foundational elements of a lasting marriage.

What happened to Zipporah by chapter 4 mirrors experiences many of us face. She was required to circumcise her child to protect the family. With a flint knife, she circumcised her son and referred to Moses as a "bridegroom of blood" (Exodus 4:26). This is significant because Zipporah was unaware of her husband's identity until the marriage was already in place. A child was already born, and now she realized circumcision, as a sign of identifying with God, was necessary.

We talk to many preacher's wives who say, "The Lord called him, not me." Zipporah shows that once you are joined in marriage, you are joined—this is now your family, your heritage, your call, your life together. Many military spouses try to remain positioned in one place while the servicemember travels the world. This separation can be unhealthy to a marriage. Even chapters later, Moses was so busy with his call that he sent Zipporah and the two sons back to her father. Jethro brought them back.

The separation occurred, but it was not meant to be a permanent way of life. So again, I ask: What is your purpose? Are we married for the concept of marriage and merely living separately? Are we married to build a shared vision? Are we married and, now that we have children, feel we may as well stay together? What is our purpose? Are we working to please God together, creating an example of how a godly relationship should thrive? If you do not know this answer, life will become increasingly frustrating, and it will be difficult to operate in unity. Creating a single sense of purpose is a collective effort.

When my marriage began, one of the things my husband said was that we would build a brick on a brick. This statement provided a collective goal. It was vague, but we learned in together to combine our efforts creating a meaning for the "Bowen" name. We coined the "circle." We agreed to raise educated, professional, law-abiding citizens. We pulled the children in a few years later and taught them what it meant to be a part of this circle and that the only way out was through death. We, as a family, came to an understanding about what the culture of our family was.

Years later, we drew a family crest. If you are married and do not know the goal, your purpose, a desired outcome, this may be a good sign to sit down and come up with a vision for your family. Include your children so they develop a sense of pride in what it means to carry on your family name and heritage. Write the vision and make it plain upon the stones.

DAY 18
Press To The Mark

I often question whether ambition can be taught. Is grit something you either have or do not have? Is there such a thing as spiritual ambition? Is there such a thing as marital ambition? Once the goal and vision are set on Day 17, Day 18 follows with establishing lines of effort to carry out those goals. Is your family Christ-centered? Is your family supportive of split vacations? Does your family expect everyone to be around to celebrate every birthday? What are the expectations? Set them and press toward the mark of the higher calling. The higher calling the Bible refers to is the greater work Jesus says we are to do.

Paul mentions this in Philippians and clearly states that he forgets the things behind him. Paul was an educated Roman who studied under Gamaliel. His intelligence and zeal positioned him to act with power and authority according to the knowledge he had of the law. In Acts 9, he had an encounter with Jesus. This encounter is like what happens in marriage: it shifts everything about our attitude, aligning both individuals to achieve the common goal of the marriage. Together, the two become one; together, they press toward the mark of the high calling of marriage.

So, if I am becoming a better wife, it is critical for me to know what the Bible says a wife should be. If I am to forget the things behind and reach for what is ahead—and what is ahead rests in Christ—my job description is clear. I forget how I used to curse out boyfriends when I was unhappy and replace it with respect for my husband, as Ephesians 5:33 instructs. I now operate with self-control and purity, representing Christ, as Titus 2 mentions.

I forget how the old me gossiped and was a busybody, replacing it with 1 Timothy 3:11 and operating in a way worthy of respect rather than malice. I become trustworthy. Ultimately, I follow the blueprint given by scripture, and I "piezo," which is Greek for press. I move forward with intense effort to reach this heavenly goal. I strive for a life aligned with the instructions in the Word of God. I focus on my established goal and do not get entangled in things that do not concern me. I set boundaries in my marriage to protect its sanctity. I operate as a faithful woman. I reflect what I believe. I do not let the actions of others impact my press. I set in my heart and mind to push forward, and I do that. I get better by working toward my goal. Some may ask, "What about when it feels like I am the only one pressing?" This is a real possibility.

I spoke with one of my dearest friends, and she reminded me of advice I had given her. She was angry because, though the advice was effective, I had not prepared her for the other person's response. That response can be so disorienting that it can knock you off your press. Do not be alarmed. Remember, each individual has free will, and since the beginning of time, God has never removed it from humanity.

The mark in the sand, the goal we are working so hard to achieve, has been established. Now for work. The press is the work. It looks difficult depending on where you sit/stand/or the position you allow yourself to see. In the military, we used to have unit tug of war. With the unit representatives on each side of the rope, once the "go" was sounded, everyone tugged with all of their might. The one team had a goal of pulling the other team over the line. The strength used to tug would shift back and forward as each team exhibited unmatched strength.

There could only be one winner in that game. In marriage, we work from the same side, and two is always better than one! We work together, and we press! If you are in a marriage and you are the only one pressing for now, keep pressing. It is highly important to have a conversation with your spouse and even seek counseling to determine if you have the same goal. Once your question is clarified, apply pressure and press! When you do not want to be loving, be loving anyway. When you do not want to cook, cook with love anyway. When you do not want to have sex or offer due benevolence (as the Bible refers to it in 1 Corinthians 7), do it with a heart of love. Even the Bible instructs us to be on one accord when deciding not to come together. Trust me, the press is better together!!

DAY 19
Caught In Adultery

You have made it to Day 19! I know you are seeing progress and refining the art of becoming a better wife. Yet being caught in the act can dismantle everything you have worked for in your marriage. Feelings of betrayal, unworthiness, and disgust fill your heart, and those emotions we discussed before overflow with intensity. The world we live in does not handle this topic well. Any human with feelings, a heart, and a sense of monogamy struggles with it. Nevertheless, we must address it.

For the sake of clarity, I will not limit this discussion to adultery—the worst violation we encounter. There are other challenges. Consider the husband who plays video games excessively, disregarding his wife. Or the husband who has struggled with pornography since his teenage years and has not broken the habit, leaving his wife feeling worthless, undervalued, and unloved.

Some spouses care more for the children than for one another. Others face illnesses that prevent intimacy, making disdain a normal part of daily life. Then there is the workaholic who will always find more hours to work or places to go, just to escape the pressures of home. And some marriages include partners who cannot speak without criticism—it is how they learned to communicate and respond.

There is a marriage with a spouse who spends recklessly and has no plan to replenish the funds. There is a marriage with a spouse who never had a parent, whose first safe love in life was absent, leaving a void they continue to search for without success. The point of Day 19 is simple: marriages have issues. Presence is a huge factor. Being physically present while never listening is still a problem.

So what is the remedy when we find ourselves in these positions? What does a married couple do to dig out of this hole? What happens when one spouse believes the other will never forgive, so they never come clean and admit the wrong? What happens when one spouse is guilt-ridden, admits it, and faces daily turmoil because of it? And what about the spouse who did not err but continues to hold the yoke of judgment on the one who did?

I use the example of the woman caught in adultery because there was no need for a jury—she was guilty. Yet the Bible does not discuss this fully in John 8. Leviticus 20:10 already declares that both the adulterer and the adulteress are to be put to death. I bring this to the forefront because in moments of pain, placing blame feels satisfying.

Assigning fault to the offender can provide a temporary sense of relief. In reality, there is always a root cause to every behavior. This chapter is not about whether you should forgive your spouse or assign fault for any other problem. Instead, I want you to know that there is a biblical way to handle issues. People often ask if they remain in good standing with God after a divorce. Jesus came so we could have life, and that life more abundantly.

The fact that He is seated at the right hand of the Father means we have access to His forgiveness. In

Matthew 19, Jesus explained that divorce was not part of the original plan, but because of the hardness of human hearts—our inability to forgive—Moses allowed certificates of divorce. Sexual unfaithfulness is a biblical ground for divorce (Matthew 5). If an unbelieving spouse leaves, that too is a ground for divorce (1 Corinthians 7:15). Many couples who face these issues for years feel ready to throw in the towel. Yet the blood of Jesus assures us that we do not have to. Some people struggle to understand how not to give up.

Many Christians facing the struggles listed above describe their marriage as having irreconcilable differences, which often reflects unforgiveness and hardened hearts. One final point for this chapter: professional counselors exist to help. God has placed psychologists and psychiatrists on the earth, some of whom offer Christian-centered practices.

On Day 19, I want you to know you are not alone. If one of the struggles above is part of your daily reality, or if you face a challenge I did not list, know that you are not alone. In addition to professional counselors, support groups exist. We are many members of one body. Often, past experiences—sometimes ones we are not even fully aware of—fuel behaviors that now play out in our marriages. And here we stand: married, and caught in the middle.

I remember the day my husband questioned me head-on about why I was a senior officer in the Army, a mother of great children who were athletic and doing wonderful things, educated and loved, yet I was sabotaging my own success. He was on the outside looking in from my perspective. Until the day he asked to come inside. When we talked, it brought to light that some things in my very own life were so suppressed that my behaviors were speaking for my traumas, and I was not invited to the conversation. Trauma runs deep; it is disturbing and distressing.

Some people can pinpoint it. Others require counseling to help it resurface so they can deal with it head-on. I did it, and it changed my life. As a pastor, I will say there are times we advocate for prayer and discourage counseling. This pastor vouches for the gift God blessed counselors with to help those of us who don't even know what to pray about. I pray this chapter removes the stigma and leads someone to help! Being a better wife acknowledges that I may need help!

DAY 20
Believe God; Make A Room

Has your faith ever caused you to act? In 2 Kings 4, there was a Shunammite woman whom the Bible never explicitly identifies as a believer, yet she recognized that a man of God would pass through. Her faith in who he was led her to seek permission from her husband to build a room for him. What we believe about someone drives how we act toward them.

If I believe I am in a relationship with a liar, my actions will naturally lead me to check phones, bank records, pockets, and more. If I believe I am with a man of God, I will act to support who he is and who he is becoming—praying for him and ensuring he has what he needs to operate effectively. Jesus asked the disciples one of the most profound questions: "Who do men say I am?" He allowed the consensus to flow through the room. As groupthink often takes hold, they answered, "Some say Elijah, some say John the Baptist, or one of the prophets." Later, in Matthew 16, He asked, "But who do you say that I am?"

If I do not believe in who my spouse is, I will act accordingly. Without a solid understanding of their identity, there is no clear point of reference. Identity is critical in marriage because the order established in Genesis 3 requires someone to lead. If the head of the marriage is unclear, how can any action follow? How can we "make a room"? Another key scripture comes from James 2: "You believe that there is one God. Good! Even the demons believe that—and shudder." Faith without understanding, without conviction, yields no action.

The scripture is powerful because it shows that faith culminates in action. Even our enemy believes and shudders at our God. What is our response?

Are we in a marriage, and because of what we see and experience, we doubt that change is possible? Do we limit what we think God can do because our spouse has acted a certain way for so long? Do we believe in God so fully that we have already made space in our living room for the quality time we are praying for? Day 20 calls for action. It is time to build a room.

It is time to define a Specific, Measurable, Achievable, Relevant, and Time-based (SMART) goal for building your room. What will the dimensions be? Will it have a balcony? What can you envision happening in your life now that you are becoming better? Now that you are being transformed daily (Romans 12:1-2) by the renewing of your mind—and resisting the thought traps of what you see or feel—how is your room coming along?

Now that you are not thinking of yourself more highly than you ought to and are preferring others above yourself, how is your room coming along? What do you want to change specifically? How will you measure it? Will it be like counting the number of kisses you place on your husband's forehead, even if he doesn't return them? Will you track the number of times you were slow to speak and considered your spouse's feelings? How will you measure this? It is critical that your goal be achievable. If the Shunammite woman had the resources of the woman at Zarephath (1 Kings 17), the story would not exist.

Your goal should also be relevant to the direction your marriage is headed, now that you have spoken with your spouse and understand your collective purpose. What is your relevant goal? Finally, establish a timeline to check your progress. Another option is to find an accountability partner—perhaps your spouse, or another couple who supports your growth—and hold one another accountable. Build your room.

Starting somewhere is better than never starting at all. Faith without works is dead. To say I want to change, I want to get better, I want to see my marriage improve and never take steps to improve it is faith without work. Let's build a room today. Who knows, we may be able to add on by this time next year. I started building my room by having simple conversations with my spouse.

I started creating spaces to be vulnerable. Initially, it was strange because it was new. Eventually, he understood that to create a safe space and a healthy conversational marriage, we—the two of us—had to create a safe space and a healthy conversational marriage. God doesn't do this part for us. Work is required. It can be done!!

DAY 21
To Moab We Go

It is Day 21. There is a story in the Bible about a woman named Naomi. Her name means pleasantness in Hebrew. Many of us share her name and her story. She followed her husband and two sons to a place called Moab, where they did not share the beliefs she was raised with. Early in the story, Naomi's husband and her sons died. Many people focus on her daughter-in-law when this story is told. I want to draw our attention instead to Naomi as we explore our final habit.

There is something to be said, especially in our time, for a woman who can follow. When I think about leadership and how it is portrayed, the emphasis is often on being in charge and taking the lead. We rarely consider that leadership requires someone to follow. Yet followership carries a negative connotation. How should we interpret this? I have a few ideas.

Before we break the story down, let's clarify a few concepts. Research identifies several types of followers: effective followers, alienated followers, sheep, yes-men, and survivors (Feist and Rosenberg, 2022). I could speak extensively about survivors, as that was my dwelling place, my personality, and my identity for a long time. Here, I want to remove any negative connotation from the word follower.

Back to Day 1, let's take control of our thoughts and consider a few possibilities. Instead of thinking negatively about followership, let's think of a group or a team. The success of the leader is inseparable from the success of the group. Without followers, there is no productivity. Without executors, no mission gets accomplished. Without help, even the most original ideas and the best plans can stall.

What does an effective follower look like exactly? She (for the sake of this book) looks like you. You might recall times when your emotions, attitude, thoughts, or feelings prevented you from following effectively. I remember those days. I remember feeling resistance in each moment, knowing I could do it my way. Usually, the resistance has a cause. Often, I think my idea is better. Sometimes, my experience or beliefs trigger a desire to take control.

Have you ever felt like this? What do you do in those moments? Here's the good news: curiosity can drive change. Moses experienced this curiosity—why is this bush burning yet not consumed? (Exodus 3:2). Like Moses, because God is no respecter of persons—meaning He can work through anyone—your curiosity can unlock your potential. The curiosity Moses exhibited led him to walk in his purpose.

Naomi followed her husband—not because it made sense, not because it was the best choice, but because he was her husband and he said they were moving. I don't want you to misunderstand: she had a voice. Many women feel compelled to speak up, speak out, or even argue against their husbands simply to be heard. Following is difficult without humility. Interestingly, after Naomi's husband and sons died, she returned home. What price do we pay when we resist being an effective follower at home? How does this bold, ungodly act affect our generation?

I wonder if she experienced times where it was hard to say what she really felt. I wonder if she ever wanted to say things and didn't speak up... I wonder if she was afraid to lie to him, so she just went with the storyline. I wonder if she thought maintaining the fragile peace made her think she would keep peace... It doesn't work like that. After 21 days of reading new ways of looking at issues and finding strength to self-improve based on God's plan for the wife, let us become committed to our relationship with the Lord, and we will see change in our marriages.

Interestingly, not every marriage ends with a happily ever after because we cannot forget each individual has their own will. God is not a God who will force anyone to change. After reading this book, you will have a closer relationship with the Father and a greater awareness of yourself!! Rinse, Wash, Repeat!! I hope you have enjoyed your journey of Becoming A Better Wife in 21 Days! It doesn't stop here. "Always becoming... never arriving (Derek Jarman)."

About The Author

Dr. Shari Bowen is a woman of faith, a devoted wife to her husband, Randy, a loving mother of six, an apostle of the gospel, a speaker, an Army veteran, and a professor by trade. She is committed to helping married women and those preparing for marriage grow spiritually while strengthening their marriages according to God's design. Through prayer, biblical wisdom, and real-life application, she equips wives to walk in love, wisdom, and purpose, both in their homes and in their relationship with God.

Drawing from her own journey of faith and marriage, Shari understands that becoming a better wife is not about striving for perfection, but about daily surrender to God. She believes that when a wife grows spiritually, it resonates throughout her life, impacting her home, her relationships, her children, and her marriage. Shari has a heart of service, and this self-help, action-oriented guide encourages wives to build strong foundations rooted in Scripture, prayer, obedience, and submission to the will of God. Her heart is to see marriages healed, communication restored, and wives empowered daily to reflect the love of Christ through humility and strength found in His Word.

Shari holds a master's degree in Organizational Psychology from Columbia University and a Doctorate in Organizational Leadership from the University of Phoenix. She has led multiple Army units, including in combat zones in Iraq and Afghanistan. Over the past four years, she taught Leadership and General Psychology at the United States Military Academy at West Point, where she earned the Dean's Early Career Diversity Award and the Teaching Excellence Award. She has also taught abroad at Management Center Innsbruck in Austria and Universidad Politecnica de Madrid (UPM) in Spain for Seton Hall.

Shari is currently an adjunct professor at Fayetteville State University. In addition to teaching, she has co-authored case studies on topics such as Psychological Safety and Managing Conflict, which have been published in Harvard Business Review, West Point's Managing Insider Risk and Organizational Journal, and other peer reviewed journals. She has spent over a decade training and mentoring leaders in both nonprofit and religious sectors in the United States as well as Grenada, West Indies.

She is also the co-founder of House of Clay International Ministries, which focuses on providing Christian education both domestically and internationally to leaders.

Acknowledgements

I first give honor to God for always guiding my steps in completing this journey. I am so grateful to my husband, Randolph G. Bowen, for inspiring this journey and being a main character forging my growth with the Lord as our marriage reaped in real time. The growth we have experienced together over the last 20 years proves just how real God is. I thank each of my children for showing me what it looks like to be proud of the product motherhood bore through submissiveness to God and compromise in parenting.

I am so proud of what each of you has become! I give a special shout out to my mother for being my very first living example of Amos 3:3; yes, ma, you demonstrated (my whole life) what it looks like for two to walk together as they agree. I thank my spiritual leaders, my bishop and first lady for the example of love and the patience during our own development. Thank you to every reader that will engage in this living document and personify the words on the page as you watch God in your own lives! Happy Reading.

References

Feist, G. J., & Rosenberg, E. L. (2022). Psychology: Perspectives and connections (5th ed.). McGraw-Hill Education.

Jarman, D. (1991). Modern nature: The journals of Derek Jarman, 1989–1990. Century

New International Version. (2011). Zondervan.

Robbins, S. P., & Judge, T. A. (2019). Organizational behavior (18th ed.). Pearson Education.

www.ingramcontent.com/pod-product-compliance
Lightning Source LLC
LaVergne TN
LVHW050843080526
838202LV00010B/323